EVERYDAY ECONOMICS

SAVING

Jessica Morrison

SECURITY SAFE

DEPOSIT

Weigl Publishers Inc.

Published by Weigl Publishers Inc.
350 5th Avenue, Suite 3304, PMB 6G
New York, NY 10118-0069

Website: www.weigl.com
Copyright ©2010 Weigl Publishers Inc.

Library of Congress Cataloging-in-Publication Data

Library of Congress Cataloging-in-Publication Data available upon request.
Fax 1-866-44-WEIGL for the attention of the Publishing Records department.

ISBN 978-1-60596-647-2 (hard cover)
ISBN 978-1-60596-648-9 (soft cover)

Printed in China
1 2 3 4 5 6 7 8 9 0 13 12 11 10 09

Project Coordinator **Heather C. Hudak** I Designer **Terry Paulhus** I Layout **Kenzie Browne**

CONTENTS

What is Saving?

Saving occurs when money is stored in a safe place and is not spent. To save money, money must be earned. Most people earn money by having jobs. By providing a service or product to others, people earn an **income** that helps them buy food, clothing, and a place to live.

Saving is possible when a person earns more money than he or she spends. This means that the income is higher than the **expenses**. Some expenses, such as food, housing, and clothing, are necessary. Items that are needed regularly are called **fixed expenses**. Sometimes, money is spent on other items, such as entertainment and eating at restaurants, but these items are not needed to survive. Understanding the difference between what is wanted and what is needed can help people save more of their money.

Shopping, eating out, and buying tickets to live shows are just some of the items people may purchase.

Budgets help people know how much money they spend compared to how much they earn. A budget details a person's fixed expenses. Any money that is left over after fixed expenses are paid can be saved. Many people decide to save a certain percentage of their income. This means they do not spend some of the money they earn.

Storing money safely is an important part of saving. Keeping money under a mattress, in a piggy bank, or in a wallet is not a good idea, as it can be lost or stolen. The safest place to keep savings is in a bank account. A **savings account** can be opened at any bank.

Sometimes , it is necessary to spend money on new clothes.

Historic Timeline of Saving

Throughout history, valuables have been saved by different cultures and people. There are many types of **currency** around the world, and the idea of saving and safekeeping money is very common.

18th-century BC Egyptians store gold in temples for safekeeping. This is one of the earliest forms of a safe.

1587 AD The Banco della Piazza di Rialto opens in Venice. Here, people can store their money in a **safety deposit box**.

1791 The First Bank of the United States is established. This is the country's first central bank. It operates until 1811.

18th-century BC   1587 AD   1791

1849 The gold rush causes many people to store their savings in banks, which are often robbed by thieves. To help prevent robberies, heavier and larger bank safes and vaults are built.

1862 The first paper money is printed in the United States.

1915 Despite a small start with a single bank, the United States has 18,227 state banks and 7,598 national banks.

1933 President Franklin Roosevelt signs the Banking Act, which also helps establish the **Federal Deposit Insurance Corporation**.

1939 The first mechanical cash dispenser is invented in New York City. Customers did not use it often, so it was removed after six months.

1958 The Bank of America launches a credit card, later known as Visa.

1967 The first electronic Automated Teller Machine (ATM) is installed in the United Kingdom.

1999 ATM **transactions** reach more than $1 billion.

21st-century Online banking becomes available. Money can be transferred between accounts and banks with the click of a mouse.

1849   1958   21st-century

Saving in the United States

Banks have been popular places to store money for hundreds of years. The world's first banks opened between the 15th and 16th centuries in Italy, Amsterdam, and Hamburg. However, one of the first banks to open in the United States was the Bank of New York. It was established in 1784. The Bank of New York is now the oldest bank in the country.

In 1933, the federal government of the United States created the Federal Deposit Insurance Corporation (FDIC). The FDIC insures the money kept in banks up to $250,000 per person. This means that, even if money is stolen from the bank, customers will not lose the money they were saving there.

During the Great Depression, people did not have much money to spend on food or clothing.

Over the years, people in the United States have gone to great extremes to save their money during financially hard times. During the Great Depression, it was common for people to patch their clothes and buy the cheapest food available.

Today, there are thousands of websites devoted to saving money and being **thrifty**. There are money management materials, such as software, to help plan budgets and spending. Some businesses help people make the best decisions for their money so they can save for their future.

FAQ

What is disposable income?
Disposable income is a term used to describe all of the money a person earns and has available to spend after taxes.

What is discretionary income?
Discretionary income is the term used to describe the money a person has available to spend after paying taxes and buying the items he or she needs to survive. Discretionary money is used to buy wanted items, such as cars and vacations.

SAVING VOCABULARY

BALANCE the amount of money in a savings account
DEPOSIT a sum of money a person puts into a savings account; putting money into an account
INTEREST a percentage of an account holder's money that a bank or organization pays the person for investing with it
LIQUID money that can be accessed to spend
PROACTIVE planning in advance for the future
WITHDRAW to remove money from a bank account

How Saving Works

One way to save money is to treat planned savings as a fixed expense. This means setting aside a certain amount of money each month as savings, much like paying a bill or buying groceries. Being **proactive** with planned savings can take some discipline, but over time, it will likely become a habit.

When saving money, people must decide where they would like to store it. Most people choose to store their money in banks. Banks pay people to store money with them. The money banks pay is known as **interest**. The bank calculates a percentage of the total **balance** of the account. This percentage is then added to the money in the account.

Interest gives the account holder a small amount of extra money just for using a bank. The amount of interest earned is based on the amount of money in the account. The more money that is stored, the more interest will be made.

In general, the longer a bank has access to the money, the higher the interest rate the account holder will receive from it.

Types of Bank Accounts

There are two main types of bank accounts that can store money.

Savings Accounts

Savings accounts are places to save and grow money. Many people store some of their money in a savings account. There are several benefits to saving money in a savings account. Funds in a savings account earn interest as incentive for a person to keep money in the bank. All general savings accounts allow account holders to **deposit** and **withdraw** money at any time. This means money is **liquid**. When money is liquid, it can easily be withdrawn as cash.

Checking Accounts

To use saved money to make purchases and other transactions, a checking account is needed. Money in a checking account earns very little interest or none at all. However, checks can be written to pay for goods and services rather than cash. Checking accounts are mainly to hold money that may be needed for spending soon.

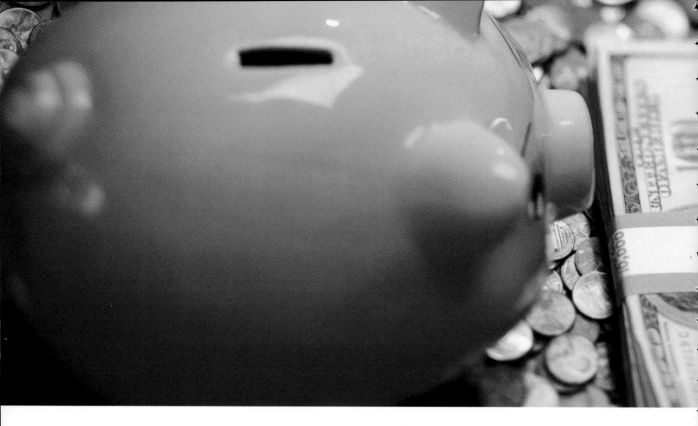

SAVING VOCABULARY

INVESTMENTS money used to buy portions of a company or organization, in hopes that it will become more valuable over time

RISK possibility of something bad happening, such as losing your money

Types of Savings Accounts

Financial institutions offer many types of savings accounts. The main difference between all savings accounts is how long money must stay in the bank, what happens to it while it is there, and how much interest it will earn.

Bank Savings Accounts

When people are just beginning to manage their money, they often are advised to make safe **investments** that have little **risk** of losing money. Bank savings accounts are quite safe because they are insured by the FDIC. A bank savings account will offer a certain amount of interest on saved money. Each bank has a different interest rate, so it is important that people do research before deciding which bank to use.

Some banks charge a small fee to store your money, though basic accounts may be free of charge.

Money Market Accounts

Money market accounts are savings accounts that pay higher interest than regular savings accounts. This can help people build their savings. However, money market accounts may require a higher minimum balance. This means there always has to be a certain amount of money in the account. This amount is normally between $1000 and $2500. Money can only be withdrawn from a money market account a few times each month.

Certificates of Deposit Accounts

A certificate of deposit (CD) is a special type of account that has a higher interest rate than most other savings accounts. This is because money cannot be withdrawn from the account for a set period of time, usually one month to five years. If money is withdrawn before this time, the account holder has to pay a penalty.

Credit Union Accounts

A credit union is like a bank, but it is owned by its members, or the people who store money there. Members help make decisions for the credit union. Credit unions are not-for-profit institutions. This means that any money a credit union earns goes back into the company or is given to members. Having a savings account at a credit union offers many of the same services as a bank. However, credit unions often provide slightly higher savings rates and lower loan rates.

Why Should You Save?

There are many reasons people decide to save their money. In general, the more money people have saved, the more they can spend on items they want. Saving money gives people the freedom to meet their financial goals and buy more expensive items. For example, if someone wants to buy a new bike that costs $100, money in a savings account can be used to buy it.

There are different types of financial goals. It usually does not take long to save enough money to buy smaller items that are not part of fixed expenses, such as a book, movie, or computer game. These are **short-term goals**. Items that cost more to purchase and take longer to save for are called **long-term goals**. Long-term goals include retirement plans, college fees, vacations, cars, and houses. These goals take more

Some people save money so they can attend college or university.

money and time to achieve, so careful saving and planning is important.

Many people save to meet short-term and long-term financial goals, as well as to have money set aside for emergencies or unexpected needs, such as losing a job or medical expenses. Having some money saved can help people deal with challenges.

Another reason to save money is to help protect against **inflation**. This refers to how the cost of items and services increases over time. Items that cost only a few dollars in the past can be very expensive today. This is because the value of the dollar has decreased over the years. As a result, it takes more money to pay for the same goods and services. For example, an item that cost $1.00 in 1913 cost $13.20 in 1990, and is more than $20.00 today.

Inflation Chart of 1913 Dollar	
Year	Equivalent of $1 over time
1913	$1.00
1930	$1.69
1945	$1.82
1960	$2.99
1975	$5.43
1990	$13.20
2005	$19.73

Behind the Scenes

What happens when withdrawing money from a teller?

As representatives of the bank, tellers are the gateway to a savings account. Tellers can help with a client's questions, and they can process simple transactions.

1. The client arrives at a bank and approaches the teller.

2. The client requests a money withdrawal.

3. The teller asks for the client's identification.

4. The teller checks the client's account balance to ensure there is enough money to cover the withdrawal.

5. The teller checks to make sure the withdrawal fits the client's savings plan.

6. The teller logs the transaction on the computer and then gives the client the money.

How an ATM works

Automated Teller Machines can save people time and help them deposit or withdraw cash safely and easily. Although the transaction at an ATM only takes a few moments to complete, there are many electronic steps to getting cash from the ATM into a person's hand.

The client places a bank card inside the ATM.

The ATM computer connects to a hosting company that sends the information from the card to a computer at the client's bank.

The client enters a number into the keypad, which is also sent to the hosting company, then to the client's bank.

The client enters transaction information using the keypad. This information is sent to the client's bank.

Once the transaction is complete, the connection between the client's bank and the ATM is stopped, and the machine returns the bank card.

A camera watches the cash as it leaves the machine. This information is logged into a journal for safekeeping.

If cash is withdrawn, it comes from a safe at the bottom or back of the ATM.

The Federal Deposit Insurance Corporation

The FDIC is a part of the federal government of the United States. It can make rules that affect banks in all 50 states. When it was first established, the FDIC was able to insure money up to $5,000. This amount increased over time to $250,000. Although the main job of the FDIC is to protect people's money, it also watches how banks work to ensure they obey the rules of their state. About 4,500 people work for the FDIC.

Banks that are protected by the FDIC will have a sign stating this inside the building. If the sign is not visible, it is a good idea to ask a banking professional before storing money at that bank. If a bank is not protected

Since the FDIC began, no one has lost money in a FDIC-insured bank.

by the FDIC, it is best not to open any accounts with it.

When money is stored in a bank, the bank is allowed to lend that money to other people. Sometimes, banks make investments with this money. If a bank loses some of its client's money in bad investments or loans that are unpaid by the borrower, the client will not lose any money. This is because the money is insured by the FDIC.

Sometimes, a bank loses so much money that it must claim **bankruptcy**. If this happens, the FDIC takes several steps to protect a client's money. First, it uses money from a large collection of money, or insurance fund, to return the money to the bank's clients. After that, the FDIC sells loans and other

assets from the failed bank to rebuild its insurance fund.

⊞FAQ

How does a person claim bankruptcy?

To claim bankruptcy, a person must file a legal document. All of the person's assets are assessed to see how much they are worth. This may include property, cars, accounts, and investments. These items are sold to pay part of the outstanding debts.

What happens after a person claims bankruptcy?

A person or company that claimed bankruptcy is no longer bound to pay its debt. However, it becomes difficult for that person or company to borrow money for future purchases. Financial institutions know the person or company has a poor record of repayment and likely will not want to take a risk.

SAVING VOCABULARY

PASS BOOK a small notebook given to a person who opens a savings account; this is used to keep track of the person's spending
PERSONAL IDENTIFICATION NUMBER (PIN) a secret number chosen when a person opens a savings account, used to access money in the person's account
RECONCILING comparing one item with another

How a Savings Account Works

Most banks offer free savings accounts for children and young adults. When choosing to open a savings account, a person needs to go to a bank and give the teller some personal information. This often includes the person's name, address, and phone number. The person also has to choose a **Personal Identification Number (PIN)**.

With this information, the teller creates an account and gives the person a bank card. This bank card can be used to access the account through a bank teller or Automated Teller Machine. If using an ATM, the PIN must be entered to prove ownership of the account and the card.

A personal identification number is required to use a debit card.

When opening a savings account, the account holder receives a **pass book**. This is a notebook in which a person records deposits and withdrawals, as well as the beginning account balance. A pass book will help a person keep track of his or her money. Although banks also track how much money is in the account, account holders are advised to make sure their records match the pass book. This is called **reconciling** the account.

Each month, statements from the bank are sent by mail or email to the account holder. This statement lists all of the transactions the account holder has made. It will show the account balance and any interest the account has earned over the month. These statements should be compared with the pass book. This can help the account holder track his or her saving and spending.

At different stages in a person's life, there will likely be a need to review the types of savings accounts this person has. Speaking with a teller or financial advisor can help a person decide the best ways to store his or her money based on current income, needs, and goals.

How to Budget

A budget is a plan for a person's or company's money. There are two basic parts to every budget. The first is to record the amount of money earned from allowances, gifts, and jobs. The second part is to record all expenses.

When budgeting, income must be compared with expenses. After listing the items that are needed and setting aside some money for the items that are wanted, the goal is to have money left over to save.

Budgets help make people aware of their spending and saving habits. Without a budget, it is easy to overspend. People also may learn they are paying more for items that could be purchased for a lesser cost. For example, a bottle of water purchased from a vending machine will likely cost more than one bought from a grocery store. **Comparison shopping** can help people decrease spending and increase saving.

Monthly Budget

Try making your own budget. First, list income you earn from jobs, gifts, or other sources for one month. Then, list all of your monthly expenses. Do you have enough money to pay for your expenses?

Monthly BUDGET

INCOME	EXPENSES
Allowance _____	Snacks _____
Gifts _____	Movies _____
Lemonade stand _____	Books _____
Babysitting _____	Video Games _____
Other _____	Other _____
_____	_____
_____	_____
_____	_____
_____	_____
Total Income $ _____	**Total Expenses $** _____

Smart Shopping

One way to save money is to become a smart shopper. When comparison shopping, the prices of similar items or the same item at different stores are compared. By looking for the best prices for similar items, people can save a great deal of money.

Comparison shopping involves reading flyers, visiting different stores, or checking prices online. Some stores have special deals or **rebates** that will save people money. Often, flyers and websites are updated every two weeks with the best prices on featured items.

Another way to save money is to ask if a store will match the price of another store carrying the same product. Sometimes, the store will give an additional discount to ensure it is purchased from it.

Clipping coupons and reading store flyers can help people get the best prices on goods and services.

Coupons are another way to save money. Many stores have weekly coupons in local flyers. There are entire websites devoted to online coupons that can be printed. Some stores offer to double a coupon's value. A coupon for $2 off shampoo at the local grocery store can save a person $4 instead.

How Does a Mail-in Rebate Work?

Customer makes a purchase from a store, paying full price for the item.

Customer mails the rebate form, receipt, and package bar code to the retailer or manufacturer offering the rebate.

The customer cashes the check or deposits it in a bank account.

The company processes the rebate application and mails a check for the rebate amount to the customer.

Saving Technology

When banks were first established, they needed a safe, strong place to store money. Before the 1920s, small safes were used to store money. Then, larger bank vaults became more popular. Bank vaults are built to fit each bank. In many cases, the bank's structure is built around the vault. Early vaults were extremely heavy, with metal walls and doors that were several feet (meters) thick. Today, bank vaults are made of concrete that is reinforced with steel. They are much smaller than earlier vaults and are 10 times stronger than concrete alone.

Engineers are constantly adding new technology to bank vaults, including heat sensors, alarms, **motion detectors**, and **eye scanners**.

Saving Careers

There are many different jobs related to saving and banking. These are just a few examples.

Division of Supervision and Customer Protection Examiners

Division of Supervision and Customer Protection (DSC) examiners work for the Federal Deposit Insurance Corporation. They ensure banks are working safely and properly. This helps protect the money people have saved at banks. Some examiners test computer systems, while others review business plans. Once a bank has been reviewed by examiners, it receives a rating. This rating helps people decide whether or not they should save their money at a particular bank. DSC examiners typically have strong analytical skills, as well as good written and verbal communication.

Certified Financial Planner

Financial planners are coaches who help people make decisions about how to save money for the future. Sometimes, financial planners help people plan for retirement, buy a home, or prepare for the expense of having children. A financial planner will look at all of a person's finances, including income, savings accounts, debt, and taxes. To become a certified financial planner, a person must be certified by the Certified Financial Planner Board of Standards. This means they have passed a 10-hour test about many areas of money planning. Financial planners often enjoy economics and math.

What Have You Learned?

1 What is a fixed expense?

2 What is the main job of the FDIC?

3 What is the difference between a checking account and a savings account?

4 What is inflation?

5 How do people reconcile a savings account?

6 What does it mean when money is liquid?

7 How should a person prioritize spending when buying things they need and things they want?

8 Who can people speak with when they have questions about opening a savings account?

9 What is one way of tracking spending to help a person save?

10 What is price matching?

Answers

1. something people must spend money on, such as house payments

2. to protect people's savings by insuring them up to $250,000

3. Checking accounts are mainly used to store money that will be spent soon. A savings account is best for money that is to be saved for a longer period of time.

4. the rising cost of living over time

5. compare the deposits with the withdrawals to ensure there are no mistakes in the pass book or in the bank records

6. It can be easily accessed and used.

7. Needs should always be purchased before wants. Saving money can help a person buy the wanted items at a later time.

8. financial advisors and tellers

9. A budget can help determine how much money is being spent. This can help people decide if they need to change their spending habits to save more money.

10. when one store matches the price of an item with the price found at another store

A Week of Saving

It takes discipline and commitment to save money. One of the best ways to do this is with a budget. Try creating a one-week budget to see how much money you can save.

1. Write the year, month, and week at the top of a sheet of paper.

2. Create a column for all of your sources of income, such as allowances, job earnings, and gifts.

3. Beside each income source, write down the amount of money you earn in one week. For example, if you receive $5 for cleaning up the yard, and you do this twice a week, write $10 beside this item on the list.

4. Add all of your weekly income amounts together, and write the total at the bottom of the column. This is how much money you make each week.

5. Now, create a column for expenses. Do you buy your lunch everyday or take a bus to school? Write out each item, and put the amount you spend in a week beside it.

6. Add all of your weekly expenses together, and write the total at the bottom of the column. This is how much money you spend each week.

7. Subtract your total expenses from your weekly income. How much money do you have left over? This money can be used to buy something you want or put into a savings account for use in the future.

Further Research

Many books and websites provide information on saving. To learn more about saving, borrow books from the library, or surf the Internet.

Most libraries have computers that connect to a database for researching information. If you input a key word, you will be provided with a list of books in the library that contain information on that topic. Nonfiction books are arranged numerically, using their call number. Fiction books are organized alphabetically by the author's last name.

Websites

Learn more about money at

www.usmint.gov/kids

Explore the ways money is protected at

**www.fdic.gov/about/learn/
learning/index.html**

Glossary

balance: the amount of money in a savings account

bankruptcy: a declaration under the law that an individual or company cannot pay its debts

budgets: careful plans for spending and saving money, based on income and expenses

comparison shopping: comparing the prices of similar items or the same item purchased at different places

currency: a unit of money that is exchanged for products or services

deposit: a sum of money a person puts into a savings account; putting money into an account

expenses: things that are bought with money

eye scanners: machines that identify people by scanning their eyes

Federal Deposit Insurance Corporation: a federal corporation that insures the money that people keep in a bank

fixed expenses: costs that do not change from month to month, such as food or transportation costs

income: the money earned from a job

inflation: the rising cost of living over time

interest: a percentage of an account holder's money that a bank or organization pays the person for investing with it

investments: money used to buy portions of a company or organization, in hopes that it will become more valuable over time

liquid: money that can be accessed to spend

long-term goals: items, such as college fees, someone wants to purchase at some time in the future or over a longer period of time

motion detectors: devices that sense movement

pass book: a small notebook given to a person who opens a savings account; this is used to keep track of the person's spending

personal identification number (PIN): a secret number chosen when a person opens a savings account, used to access money in the person's account

proactive: planning in advance for the future

rebates: offers from a company to receive a certain amount of money back after your purchase

reconciling: comparing one item with another

risk: possibility of something bad happening, such as losing your money

safety deposit box: a small box used to store valuables; located inside a bank

savings account: a bank account for money that is being saved

short-term goals: items, such as a video game, someone wants to purchase relatively soon

thrifty: careful with money

transactions: acts of business, such as withdrawing or depositing money in a bank account

withdraw: to remove money from a bank account

Index